INTEGRITY RISKS AND RED FLAGS IN
AGRICULTURE, NATURAL RESOURCES, AND RURAL DEVELOPMENT PROJECTS

JANUARY 2023

ADB

ASIAN DEVELOPMENT BANK

© 2023 Asian Development Bank
6 ADB Avenue, Mandaluyong City, 1550 Metro Manila, Philippines
Tel +63 2 8632 4444; Fax +63 2 8636 2444
www.adb.org

Some rights reserved. Published in 2023.

ISBN 978-92-9269-991-8 (print); 978-92-9269-992-5 (electronic)
Publication Stock No. SGP220600-2
DOI: http://dx.doi.org/10.22617/SGP220600-2

The views expressed in this publication are those of the authors and do not necessarily reflect
the views and policies of the Asian Development Bank (ADB) or its Board of Governors or
the governments they represent.

ADB does not guarantee the accuracy of the data included in this publication and accepts no
responsibility for any consequence of their use. The mention of specific companies or products
of manufacturers does not imply that they are endorsed or recommended by ADB in preference to
others of a similar nature that are not mentioned.

By making any designation of or reference to a particular territory or geographic area, or by using
the term "country" in this publication, ADB does not intend to make any judgments as to the legal
or other status of any territory or area.

Please contact pubsmarketing@adb.org if you have questions or comments with respect to
content, or if you wish to obtain copyright permission for your intended use that does not fall within
these terms, or for permission to use the ADB logo.

Corrigenda to ADB publications may be found at http://www.adb.org/publications/corrigenda.

Notes:
References in this publication to bidders, bids, bid evaluation committees, and bid evaluation
reports are used within the context of the procurement of works (contractors), goods (suppliers),
and consulting and non-consulting services.

All photos by ADB except when otherwise stated.

In this publication, "$" refers to United States dollars.

On the cover: **Farming in the Philippines**. An elderly Filipino farmer weeds his rice field in
Lucban, Quezon (photo by Al Benavente).

Cover design by Paolo Tan.

CONTENTS

TABLES, FIGURE, BOX, AND CHECKLISTS

TABLES

FIGURE

BOX

CHECKLISTS

FOREWORD

Since 2003, the Asian Development Bank's Office of Anticorruption and Integrity has conducted proactive integrity reviews (PIRs) to identify and address control weaknesses that give rise to integrity risks in ongoing sovereign operations. Insights from these PIRs are published in this series, *Integrity Risks and Red Flags*.

This publication highlights weaknesses and red flags identified through PIRs of 14 agriculture, natural resources, and rural development projects financed by ADB. Further volumes in the series feature insights from five other sectors: education, energy, health, transport, and water. Through this sector-based series, governments, public bodies, and stakeholders engaged in designing and implementing projects can learn from past vulnerabilities and establish processes and controls to effectively mitigate integrity risks.

To help foster and sustain economic growth, ADB's Strategy 2030 underscores the strengthening of governance and institutional capacity as an operational priority in the bank's developing member countries. Let us achieve a prosperous, inclusive, resilient, and sustainable Asia and the Pacific by maintaining the highest ethical standards.

John Versantvoort
Head, Office of Anticorruption and Integrity
Asian Development Bank

ACKNOWLEDGMENTS

Integrity Risks and Red Flags in Agriculture, Natural Resources, and Rural Development Projects was prepared and developed collaboratively by H. Lorraine Wang (former advisor), Caridad Garrido Ortega (consultant and former senior integrity specialist), and Erickson M. Quijano (consultant) of the Preventive and Compliance Division, Office of Anticorruption and Integrity, Asian Development Bank.

This publication greatly benefited from the insights and comments of John Versantvoort (head), David Binns (former advisor), Lisa Kelaart-Courtney (director), Jung Min Han (senior integrity specialist), and Kristopher Marasigan (integrity officer) of the Office of Anticorruption and Integrity. This publication was made possible by reviews from Lance Gore (principal portfolio management specialist, South Asia Department), Yasmin Siddiqi (director, Central and West Asia Department), Michiko Katagami (principal natural resources and agriculture specialist, Sustainable Development and Climate Change Department [SDCC]), Hanif Rahemtulla (principal public management specialist, SDCC), and Alaysa Escandor (public management officer – Governance, SDCC).

ABBREVIATIONS

ADB	Asian Development Bank
ANR	agriculture, natural resources, and rural development
BEC	bid evaluation committee
OAI	Office of Anticorruption and Integrity
PIR	proactive integrity review

INTRODUCTION

Since the Asian Development Bank (ADB) adopted its Anticorruption Policy in 1998, fighting corruption has become embedded in ADB's broader work in governance, public administration, and capacity development.[1] The Anticorruption Policy affirms the bank's zero tolerance for corruption and lays the groundwork for supporting anticorruption efforts.

ADB's Strategy 2030 identifies strengthening governance and institutional capacity as one of seven operational priorities for a prosperous, inclusive, resilient, and sustainable Asia and the Pacific. The Office of Anticorruption and Integrity (OAI) promotes the implementation of this operational priority through a combination of activities aimed at (i) enforcement and (ii) prevention and compliance.

The proactive integrity review (PIR) is a mechanism used by ADB since 2003 to help prevent and detect integrity violations and address risks in ADB-financed or -administered projects. PIRs (i) identify and assess integrity risks in procurement, contract and asset management, and financial management of a project; and (ii) recommend measures to mitigate these risks and ensure that project funds are used for their intended purposes.

PIRs evaluate the adherence of projects to three core principles of project integrity: (i) transparency—proper documentation of key decisions, public disclosure of project information, and protection of confidential information; (ii) fairness—objective and reliable bidding process and requirements optimizing competition, impartial evaluation, and a credible complaints mechanism; and (iii) accountability and control—accurate and timely project accounting and reporting, eligibility of expenditures and timely payments, adherence to contract provisions, and adequate project oversight and management.

OAI ensures that PIR knowledge is applied to the projects reviewed through follow-up reviews, at which time OAI verifies the implementation status of the PIR. In addition, OAI assists the executing and implementing agencies in addressing open recommendations.[2]

PIR knowledge is institutionalized in ADB operations through (i) embedding of PIR requirements in ADB guidance and instruction documents, (ii) integrity risk management reviews, (iii) knowledge enhancement and transfer workshops and other learning courses, and (iv) knowledge products.[3] Following a country-focused approach (one of three guiding principles outlined in Strategy 2030), PIR knowledge also informs the country partnership strategies of developing member countries.[4] Through this exercise, PIR knowledge is considered in designing new projects as the country partnership strategy predominantly drives country operations business plans.

This publication presents vulnerabilities from PIRs of 14 agriculture, natural resources, and rural development (ANR) projects (Appendix) across 12 countries and 4 regions and highlights recommended measures to mitigate identified integrity risks.[5]

---

[1] ADB. 1998. *Anticorruption Policy*. Manila.

[2] The follow-up review reports document the implementation status of PIR recommendations (footnote 5).

[3] Through integrity risk management reviews, PIR knowledge is built in preapproval project documents (concept papers, reports and recommendations of the President to the Board of Directors, technical assistance reports).

[4] The country partnership strategy is the primary platform for defining ADB's operational focus in a developing member country.

[5] The ANR projects reviewed were selected from all active ADB-financed loan and grant projects using a risk-based selection process. The selection process considered the size of funding, lending modality, implementation arrangements, number of awarded contracts, level of disbursements, inputs from relevant ADB departments, prior project results, external benchmarking, and potential benefits of a PIR to the project. PIR reports are available on the ADB website (*https://www.adb.org/who-we-are/integrity/proactive-integrity-review*).

SECTOR OVERVIEW

ADB's efforts and strategy in promoting rural development and food security are outlined in the Operational Plan for Sustainable Food Security in Asia and the Pacific.[6]

Under the plan, ADB has shifted its strategic focus from agriculture to a comprehensive multisector food security engagement approach with the goal of curbing food insecurity, particularly among the poor and vulnerable. ADB will help transform agriculture and food supply systems to increase farmers' income, enable consumers' access to safe and nutritious food, and stimulate economic activity in rural areas. The plan also highlights ADB's role in promoting rural development by improving connectivity and services, establishing agriculture value chains with market infrastructure, and enhancing food security through better irrigation, farm inputs, and capacity building.

Table 1 presents ADB's financial resources commitments in the ANR sector from 2017 to 2021.

Table 1: ADB's Financing Commitments in the Agriculture, Natural Resources, and Rural Development Sector, 2017–2021

YEAR	2017	2018	2019	2020	2021
Value ($ million)	1,546	2,375	2,309	1,281	1,490
Percent of commitments in all sectors	7.10%	9.69%	9.61%	4.06%	6.55%

Source: ADB. 2022. ADB Annual Report 2021. Manila.

---

[6] ADB. 2015. *The Operational Plan for Agriculture and Natural Resources: Promoting Sustainable Food Security in Asia and the Pacific in 2015–2020*. Manila.

INTEGRITY RISKS AND RED FLAGS

Methodology

OAI identified and synthesized integrity-related vulnerabilities, including red flags, from its ANR PIR findings.[7] A vulnerability is any gap in a project's implementation processes that, if not remedied in a timely manner, will increase the likelihood of an integrity violation occurring and/or the impact of an integrity violation. In other words, the vulnerability increases the risk profile of the project.

Integrity risk is the risk that project funds are diverted from their intended purposes due to fraud, corruption, or other integrity violations.[8] Integrity violations are more likely to occur if integrity risks are not detected or not addressed effectively in a timely manner. Integrity risk management is an essential prerequisite for ensuring that projects achieve the intended development outcomes.

OAI assessed the level of vulnerabilities (high, medium, or low) by occurrence and impact.[9] This publication follows the project implementation processes and related subprocesses shown in Table 2. It also describes high- and medium-risk vulnerabilities and mitigating measures in each project implementation process.

Table 2: Project Implementation Processes

Process		
Procurement	**Contract and Asset Management**	**Financial Management**

Subprocess		
A1 Bidding Prequalification, bidding documents preparation, bid advertisements, submissions, and opening	**B1 Contract administration** The management of the day-to-day practicalities and administrative requirements under the contract	**C1 Expenditure management** Approval and processing of payments for project expenditures
A2 Bid evaluation Assessment of bidders' compliance with bidding requirements, and preparation and approval of evaluation report	**B2 Output monitoring** Engagement with and/or supervision of contractors, consultants, and suppliers in relation to project outputs	**C2 Financial reporting** Project accounting and auditing
A3 Contract award Post-bid evaluation activities until contract is awarded and signed	**B3 Asset control** Safeguarding and maintenance of project assets including asset inventory	

Note: The subprocesses reflect those prioritized by the Office of Anticorruption and Integrity and do not reflect all subprocesses that exist within each process.
Source: Office of Anticorruption and Integrity, Asian Development Bank.

---

[7] Red flags are indicators of irregularities, which may indicate the occurrence of integrity violations. Project staff should be alert to red flags of integrity violations for them to promptly report potential violations to OAI.

[8] Integrity violation is any act which violates ADB's Anticorruption Policy, including corrupt, fraudulent, coercive, or collusive practice; abuse; conflict of interest; and obstructive practice. Other integrity violations include violations of ADB sanctions, retaliation against whistleblowers and witnesses, and other violations of ADB's Anticorruption Policy, including failure to adhere to the highest ethical standards.

[9] OAI determined the occurrence of a vulnerability by establishing the frequency with which this was identified in the PIRs; and based the impact of a vulnerability on the likelihood that this could have resulted in an integrity violation or misuse of project funds.

Integrity Risk Heat Maps

The heat map in Figure (a) shows the level of risk arising from vulnerabilities identified in ANR PIRs and presented in the processes in which they manifested.[10] In the 14 ANR projects reviewed, OAI identified high integrity risks in all processes, i.e., procurement, contract and asset management, and financial management.

Figure (b) shows the risk level by subprocess. Risk levels are highest in bidding (A1), bid evaluation (A2), output monitoring (B2), expenditure management (C1), and financial reporting (C2) subprocesses.

Figure: Integrity Risk Heat Maps

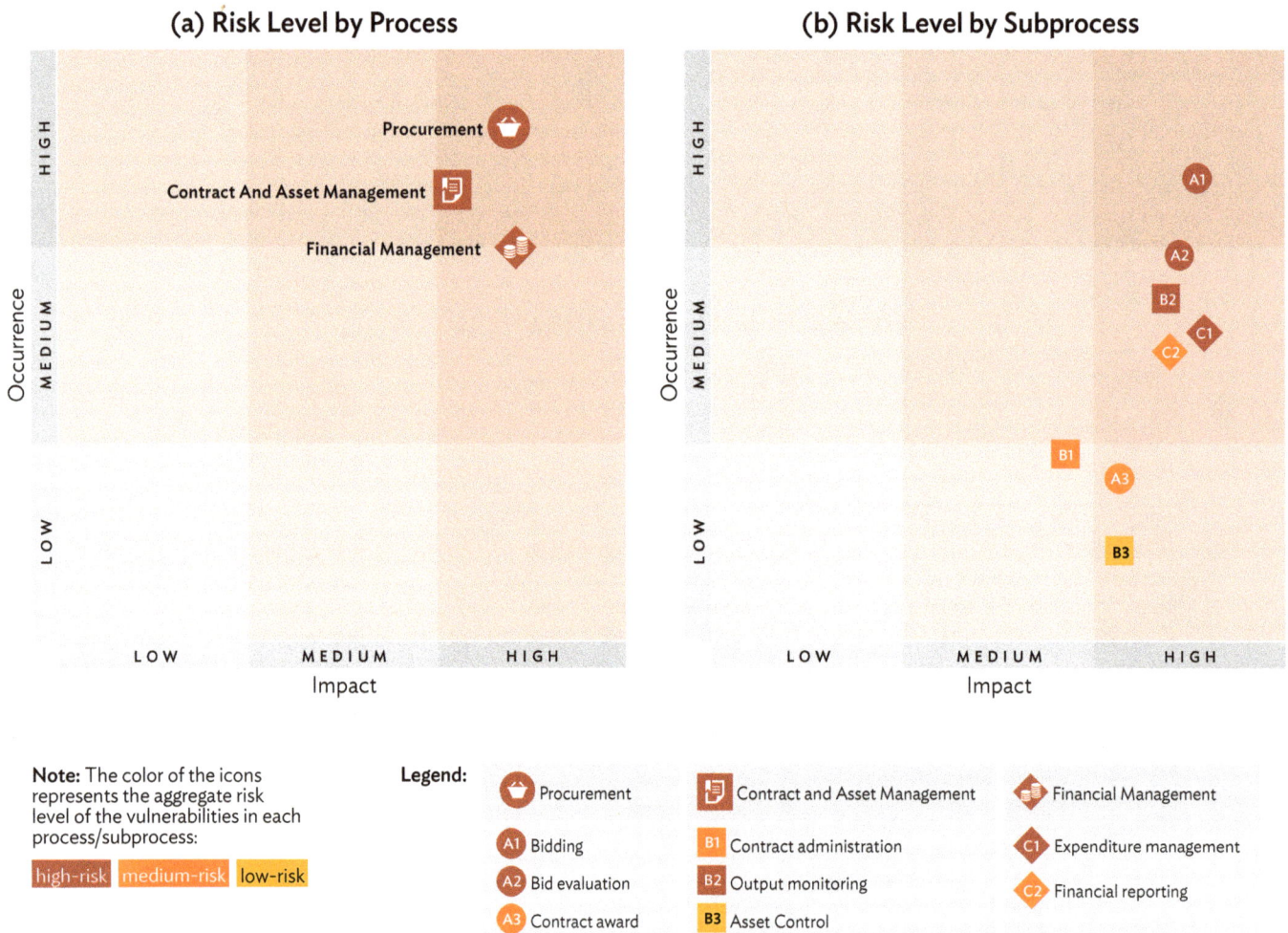

(a) Risk Level by Process

(b) Risk Level by Subprocess

Note: The color of the icons represents the aggregate risk level of the vulnerabilities in each process/subprocess:

high-risk   medium-risk   low-risk

Legend:

- Procurement
- Contract and Asset Management
- Financial Management
- A1 Bidding
- B1 Contract administration
- C1 Expenditure management
- A2 Bid evaluation
- B2 Output monitoring
- C2 Financial reporting
- A3 Contract award
- B3 Asset Control

Source: Office of Anticorruption and Integrity, Asian Development Bank.

---

[10] The heat map is a visual representation of relationships among two sets of data: the likelihood that an integrity violation may occur (occurrence) and its potential impact to the project (impact).

Vulnerabilities and Mitigating Measures

OAI's analysis aimed to identify factors contributing to integrity vulnerabilities and to formulate risk mitigating measures. These measures may be applied to all projects regardless of their financing modality or structure. Project teams can use the due diligence checklists during bid evaluation (Checklist 1) and expenditure payment processing (Checklist 2) to identify and mitigate integrity risks.[11]

PROCUREMENT

(A1) Bidding

Red flags indicative of integrity violations. OAI identified red flags indicating that the fairness of the bidding process may have been undermined. These increase the likelihood of occurrence of fraud and corruption that may jeopardize the project and alienate prospective bidders. Examples of red flags in bidding are summarized in Table 3.

Red flags are multifaceted, and those summarized in Table 3 may have one or a combination of the elements of collusion, fraud, corruption, and/or conflicts of interest.

Table 3: Examples of Red Flags in Bidding

Type of Integrity Violation	Red Flags
Collusive practice	**"Lost" bids** The project management office could not provide procurement documents (e.g., bids, feasibility studies, bid attendance records) to support the bid evaluation reports. Moreover, the project management office forwarded the bid evaluation report to ADB at least a year after the biddings took place.
	Unreasonably narrow contract specifications Specifications appeared to be unreasonably narrow, which resulted in the project liaison office purchasing 17 pick-up trucks from one vendor at above-market prices. This also reduced competition because bidders that could possibly have offered market-based prices for trucks of equivalent or better quality did not participate in the bidding process.
	Similarities in bids • Bids contained almost identical technical proposals, including layout and writing, except for the price. In one case, the losing bidders requested that their bid securities be refunded to the winning bidder to cover the cost of its performance security. • A winning and losing bidder submitted sequential bid securities issued by the same bank. In addition, traces of the winning bidder's signature in the bid document were identified in the losing bid. Attempts to conceal the signature had been made using correction fluid.

continued on next page

---

[11] OAI rolled out project management checklists to help executing and implementing agencies to self-assess (i) executing/implementing agency capacity, (ii) project procurement processes, (iii) financial management, and (iv) project output management from an integrity perspective. These checklists are available at https://www.adb.org/who-we-are/integrity/proactive-integrity-review.

Table 3 *continued*

Type of Integrity Violation	Red Flags
Collusive practice *(continued)*	**Bid to lose** Bids, which were clearly inferior or grossly deficient, were submitted by bidders to give the impression that the bid process was competitive. Examples include the bidder proposing irrelevant work methods and omitting essential documents from the bids, such as bid securities.
	Limited number of bidders submitted bids Among 86 contractors prequalified for civil works contracts, only 3–5 contractors bid for each contract.
	Bidders submitted identical line item bid amount Bills of quantities in 20 out of 28 civil works contracts contained line item prices that were identical to other bids (seen in 12 contracts) or to the engineer's cost estimates (observed in eight contracts) despite the engineer's cost estimates not being publicly disclosed.
	Apparent connections between bidders and/or common addresses, personnel, phone numbers, etc. Bidders across six contracts were related parties, and their bids contained similarities in addresses, directors, officers, and management (also conflict of interest).
	Lack of verifiable contact information (indicative of phantom vendors) In one instance, the address of a losing bidder did not exist. For another, the bidder used a travel agency's address.
	Inadequate or apparently altered documentation The bills of quantities under four civil works contracts contained handwritten corrections, which the bidder or bid evaluation committee might have made. The party responsible for making the corrections could not be established due to the unavailability of original bills of quantities or documented explanation/s for such changes.
Conflict of interest	**Incompatible functions performed by a single person** Without independent verification, provincial engineers performed incompatible functions such as authenticating certificates of project advancement and endorsing checks to contractors. Because provincial engineers generally have full control over all aspects of work design and completion, the conflict of interest may have hampered the detection of subproject design deficiencies and the prevention of inappropriate payment processing.
	Close associations with a vendor In two cadastral survey work biddings, the bid evaluation committee failed to disqualify a firm earlier disqualified on the grounds that the implementing agency's project manager used to work for that firm, i.e., conflict of interest with the project manager (also collusive practice).

Notes: 1. Collusive practice is an arrangement between two or more parties designed to achieve an improper purpose, including influencing improperly the actions of another party.

2. Fraudulent practice is any act or omission, including a misrepresentation, that knowingly or recklessly misleads, or attempts to mislead, a party to obtain a financial or other benefit or to avoid an obligation.

3. Conflict of interest is any situation in which a party has interests that could improperly influence a party's performance of official duties or responsibilities, contractual obligations, or compliance with applicable laws and regulations.

Source: Office of Anticorruption and Integrity, Asian Development Bank.

Box: Potential Collusive Practices in the Bidding of a Decentralized Project

The overall goal of the decentralized project was to reduce rural poverty in 18 very poor remote hill and mountain districts affected by conflict in a Southeast Asian developing member country. The proactive integrity review (PIR) noted red flags that strongly suggested the occurrence of collusion during the procurement of 28 contracts worth about $1.5 million in 6 of 18 districts.

Limited number of bidders. In 70% of contracts reviewed where more than 20 contractors purchased bid documents, the level of participation was low, ranging from 9% to 22%. In one of the districts, only one bidder submitted bids for Lots 1–14 out of a number of bidders that purchased bidding documents. Pre-bid meetings could not be held due to lack of attendance by any of the bidders. In two other districts, none of the bidders attended the bid opening. In a contract with three participating bidders, the two losing bidders did not submit mandatory requirements, which caused their disqualification. Given these circumstances, it appeared that bids were manipulated to ensure that contracts were awarded to the predetermined winner.

Similarities in bids. In one of the contracts, the bills of quantities of the winning bidder and one of the losing bidders had similarities in handwriting style and text. In another contract, the certifications on availability of equipment to be leased for the winning bidder and one of the losing bidders were identical in text and format, although written using different letterheads. These appeared to have been filled out by the same person. In another contract, three bidders quoted similar unit prices for 72% of the bills of quantities' items.

Apparent connections between bidders. Competing related bidders were prevalent for contracts in three districts. In one district, three winning bidders that competed against each other for three separate contracts all had the same registered address and directors. In another district, where only two bidders submitted bids for a civil works contract, the directors of the two firms had familial relations, as uncle and nephew. In another district, where three suppliers submitted quotations, the winning supplier and one of the losing suppliers had the same shareholders and the same telephone numbers listed in their bids.

Bidders submitted identical and/or similar line item bid amounts. About 55% of the line items quoted by the winning bidder in one of the districts were identical to the engineer's cost estimates. Losing bidders also had similar quotations to that of the cost estimates in respect of certain items. The differences in unit rates between the cost estimates and quoted rates among bidders were minimal.

Vendors not in business or in telephone directories or with inadequate identification information (also known as phantom vendors). In two contracts awarded to the same vendor, the address of the losing bidder was that of a travel agency, which indicated the existence of a possible phantom bidder. In another contract, the address of a losing bidder was nonexistent. These indicate the possible use of phantom bidders to give an impression of a competitive procurement process.

TAKEAWAY

Increasing project supervision and monitoring mechanisms are crucial for highly decentralized project implementation, as such projects are particularly prone to potential integrity violations infiltrating the procurement process.

Source: Office of Anticorruption and Integrity, Asian Development Bank.

MITIGATING MEASURES
Red Flags of Integrity Violations

- ADB regional departments and resident missions should ensure that executing and implementing agencies, including project implementing units/offices and evaluation committees, understand their obligations under ADB's Anticorruption Policy, especially the obligation to report any integrity violation to OAI when such allegation is initially identified or suspected. Executing and implementing agencies should communicate these obligations to the bidders (contractors, consultants, suppliers), provide the necessary oversight, and conduct appropriate due diligence to minimize the risk of integrity violations on development projects.

- The executing agency should (i) establish procedures for all executing and implementing agency staff to disclose real or perceived conflict of interest with any bidders or other parties involved in the project and (ii) actively monitor staff integrity and require staff to adhere to the highest ethical standards.

Deficiencies in bidding document sales and bid submission registers. These diminish the transparency and fairness of the bidding process. Particularly, these may result in a potential bidder not receiving important bidding information, thereby causing an otherwise qualified bidder not to be considered in the bid evaluation. Also, in the absence of these registers (or deficient information thereof), it would be difficult to ascertain (i) how, when, and by whom bids were submitted; (ii) whether all parties were provided the same information; and (iii) whether bids were submitted within the advertised deadline. Examples of this vulnerability are summarized in Table 4.

Table 4: Examples of Deficiencies in Bidding Document Sales and Bid Submission Registers

Item	Nature of Deficient Information
Bidding document sales	A total of nine bidding documents were sold but only eight names of bidders were recorded in the register. The name of the bidder that was not recorded was one of the two bidders that submitted bids.
Bid submission	• The project management office did not maintain registers to track requests for proposals, bids, and quotations, including those received for shopping contracts. • The names and signatures of persons submitting the bids were not captured in the bid submission register. • A bid for a civil works package was not recorded in the bid submission register.

Source: Office of Anticorruption and Integrity, Asian Development Bank.

MITIGATING MEASURES
Deficiencies in Bidding Document Sales and Bid Submission Registers

The executing and implementing agencies should improve the controls relating to the purchase of bids and issuance of receipts. This should include accurate record keeping, including registers for sales of bidding documents and bid submissions. The registers should contain information that could facilitate ascertaining, at a minimum, (i) how, when, and by whom bids were sold and submitted; (ii) whether all parties were provided the same information; and (iii) whether bids were submitted within the advertised deadline.

Deficient and inconsistent information in the bidding documents. Without clear and consistent requirements in the bidding documents, the evaluation may be subjective and prone to errors. If not mitigated, evaluation errors may lead to the selection of unqualified bidders, thereby exposing the project to losses. Examples of this vulnerability are summarized in Table 5.

Table 5: Examples of Deficient and Inconsistent Information in the Bidding Documents

Bidding Requirement/ Aspect	Nature of Deficient/Inconsistent Information
Technical specifications	• The technical specifications for the purchase of a copier were not clearly defined in the bidding documents, hence, bidders proposed copiers with different capacities. • A specific brand name which was identifiable to the winning bidder (the lone bidder) in an international competitive bidding contract was included in the technical specifications for a bidding.
Required undertaking	The letter of bid template did not include an undertaking by the contractor that no fees, gratuities, rebates, gifts, commissions, or other payments, except those shown in the bid, were given or received in connection with the procurement process or in contract execution.
Scoring	The executing agency added unnecessary sub-criteria that may have favored certain bidders (e.g., 5 points for having a letter of promise to provide capital).

Source: Office of Anticorruption and Integrity, Asian Development Bank.

MITIGATING MEASURES
Deficient and Inconsistent Information in the Bidding Documents

• The executing and implementing agencies should (i) refer to ADB's guidance notes on procurement during the preparation of the bidding documents and (ii) provide clear and consistent information in the bidding documents to enable bidders to prepare responsive bids.

• The regional departments should (i) thoroughly review the draft bidding documents submitted by executing and implementing agencies to ensure accuracy of required information and (ii) report any potential integrity violations to OAI when such allegations are initially identified or suspected.

(A2) Bid Evaluation

Vulnerabilities in bid evaluation can result in contracts awarded to unqualified bidders, thereby undermining the transparency and fairness of the procurement at an ultimate cost to the project. Process inconsistencies and deficiencies, and inaccurate evaluation results may create the impression of favoring bidders. If not addressed, these vulnerabilities may eventually lead to substandard outputs, delayed implementation, waste, loss of funds, or harm to the intended beneficiaries.

Inadequate due diligence. Bidders may provide dubious information on their eligibility, financial capacity, and experience. Without adequate due diligence during bid evaluation, bid evaluation committees (BECs) may fail to identify irregularities, inconsistencies, and/or potential misrepresentation.

Following a risk-based approach, the BEC should conduct due diligence to verify the submitted bid information against supporting documents (records check), from online sources (sanctions and other desktop research including previous adverse news), and/or from third parties (reference check). Combined with professional attributes such as a questioning mind and a critical assessment of documents, due diligence requires looking for indications of errors/misrepresentations on the documents, including checking the accuracy of information drawn from computations. The BEC should also seek clarifications/substantiation from bidders to the extent allowed by the bidding documents.

Examples of these evaluation errors resulting from the lack of, or inadequate due diligence are summarized in Table 6.

Table 6: Examples of Evaluation Errors

Bid Evaluation Aspect/Requirement	Nature of Evaluation Error
Financial capacity	• A bidder's letter of credit did not show the available/unutilized balance, yet the bidding evaluation committee (BEC) considered the credit line's total amount. The BEC did not seek clarification from the bidder to establish the portion of the credit line that may be considered for evaluation purposes. • The BEC incorrectly included fixed assets as a component of a bidder's available financial resources. • The BEC did not identify the discrepancies between the cash and cash equivalents in the bid form, which exceeded the current assets in the bidder's audited financial statements.
Equipment	The winning bidder submitted an equipment list that was prepared 6 years prior to the bid submission. BEC's validation of the existence of the equipment in the list could not be ascertained.
Eligibility	• The BEC did not request for clarification when the winning bidder submitted a tax identification number certificate but did not submit the required income certificate. • The BEC did not detect that the supplier's name on the submitted company license differed from the name in the quotation. The legitimacy of the supplier's business was therefore unconfirmed at the time of the contract award.
Experience	• The trade license of the second lowest bidder for a works contract pertained to steel re-rolling and cement supply and not for construction business, as required in the bidding documents. However, the BEC declared the bidder as responsive. • The BEC declared a winning bidder compliant with the experience requirement even though the bidder's experience was on building construction (with no supporting documents) instead of the required road construction experience. The bidder cited experience in the construction of a three-level multistoried car park and winding driveway inside the car park. This work experience was inadequate for the large-scale road construction contract being bid out. ⚠
General	The BEC accepted bids, including the winning bids, even though the following deficiencies were noted: ⚠ • Bid application letter was signed by personnel other than the legal representative of the bidders (i.e., the director) without proper authorization letter attached. • Key details, especially, financial data were misstated/absent. • Bids were not initialed on all pages. • Discount letters were not dated or dated after the bid opening date. • Signatures of bidders' key personnel on their curriculum vitae as attached to the bid proposal appeared to be forged. • Financial information provided by the bidders was not certified or audited. The BEC removed a bidder based on a letter of withdrawal without first confirming its authenticity. The letter was later confirmed to include fake signatures, company stamp, and letterhead.

Legend: ⚠ = red flag of bid manipulation (collusive practice). Collusive practice is an arrangement between two or more parties designed to achieve an improper purpose, including influencing improperly the actions of another party.

Source: Office of Anticorruption and Integrity, Asian Development Bank.

⚒ **MITIGATING MEASURES**
Vulnerabilities in Bid Evaluation

- BEC members should undergo detailed and practical hands-on training on all aspects of bid evaluation, especially due diligence, before undertaking new bid evaluation assignments. Support from ADB regional departments, supervision consultants, and engaged procurement experts is required (a checklist on how to avoid common errors and/or lapses in bid evaluation is on Checklist 1).

- ADB regional departments should perform rigorous reviews of bid evaluation reports, particularly when the executing agency's procurement capacity is not robust or when contracts are high value, high risk, or complex. Rigorous review entails seeking clarifications from the executing and implementing agencies, calling in bids on a sample basis, validating evaluation report information against bids, and assessing the reasonableness of significant evaluation committee decisions.

Checklist 1: How to Avoid Common Errors and Lapses in Bid Evaluation

ADB Sanctions List
☐ Verify that the bidder (all parties to the joint venture/association/consortium agreement) is not on ADB's complete Sanctions List (https://sanctions.adb.org).

Construction Turnover
☐ Verify the turnover declared on the bidding form against the turnover reported in the audited financial statements submitted.

Financial Capacity
☐ Verify the financial capacity-related accounts (working capital, net worth) declared on the bidding form against the corresponding accounts in the audited financial statements submitted.

☐ Verify the credit lines declared against the supporting documents submitted.

Current Contract Commitments
☐ Verify the current contract commitments declared on the bidding form against the contract commitments reported in the audited financial statements submitted.

Experience
☐ Verify the experience declared in the bidding form against the work completion certificates (for works) and curricula vitae (for experts and consultants) submitted.

Pending Litigation
☐ Verify the pending litigations declared on the bidding form against the pending litigation disclosures in the audited financial statements submitted.

Criteria Requiring Computations
☐ Recompute the amounts on the bidding forms and verify that the formula used, including the exchange rates, are correct.

ADB = Asian Development Bank, OAI = Office of Anticorruption and Integrity.
Note: Where a red flag is identified, refer it to OAI for further verification.
Source: Office of Anticorruption and Integrity, Asian Development Bank.

⒜ Contract Award

Deficient performance securities. Deficient performance securities result in non-protection to the executing agency in case of breach of contract by the contractor and/or supplier. They heighten the risk of increased project cost and implementation delays. Examples of deficiencies include performance security amounts that are lower than the contract requirement and performance securities with validity dates ending within the contract period.

PROCUREMENT

CONTRACT
AND ASSET
MANAGEMENT

MITIGATING MEASURES
Lack of Standard Accountability
Provisions in Contracts

The executing and/or implementing agencies should strictly enforce the performance security requirements. In cases of delay in the delivery of goods or completion of services, the contractor and/or supplier should be requested to appropriately extend the validity period of the performance security.

CONTRACT AND ASSET MANAGEMENT

B1 Contract Administration

Deficient securities and insurance. If contractors and suppliers do not provide adequate performance securities and required insurance coverage, the executing agency has no recourse if (i) project assets are damaged or lost (including injury or death of the workers); and (ii) the supplier/contractor does not fulfill its obligations, thereby jeopardizing the project's development objectives. Examples of these deficiencies are in Table 7.

Table 7: Examples of Deficiencies in Securities and Insurance

Item	Security/Insurance Deficiency
Insurance	• The project management unit did not impose contract requirements for adequate insurance on liquidated damages. • The contractors did not provide insurance coverage for laborers for all civil works contracts (national competitive bidding) reviewed.
Advance payment security	• The winning consultancy firm submitted an advance payment security that had expired before the full advance recoupment. • The project management unit did not obtain an advance payment security from the contractor.

Source: Office of Anticorruption and Integrity, Asian Development Bank.

MITIGATING MEASURES
Deficient Securities and
Insurance

• The executing and/or implementing agencies should (i) obtain adequate insurance from contractors and/or suppliers, including the corresponding insurance certificates containing complete information in terms of validity period, correct beneficiary, and description of coverage; (ii) obtain adequate advance payment security from contractors; and (iii) strictly enforce the performance security requirements.

• In cases of delay in the delivery of goods or completion of services, the contractor and/or supplier should be requested to appropriately extend the validity period of the insurance, bank guarantee, or performance security (which should include the warranty period), where relevant.

B2 Output Monitoring

Deficiencies in the reporting of project's implementation progress. This lack of transparency results in implementation complications, especially delays and poor-quality outputs not being addressed in a timely manner. Examples of deficiencies in progress reporting are summarized in Table 8.

Table 8: Examples of Deficiencies in Progress Reporting

Progress Reporting Aspect	Deficiency
Reporting system	There was no management information system that recorded the details and status of the overall project, including for each subproject at the district level. Records that appropriately reflect the contracts and their status, e.g., completed or in progress, per district were not readily available at the project implementation unit.
Quality of reports	• Construction diaries were not adequately maintained by contractors and reviewed by supervision consultants. In some cases, information presented in the diaries was either incomplete or incorrect, or construction diaries were missing.

	• The supervision consultant submitted quarterly progress reports that were deficient in the following aspects:
	  › Lack of contract references necessary to identify the exact location of the sites, sections of works covered, and the contractor responsible for the works;
	  › Inadequate information on project implementation issues and corresponding corrective actions taken, other than with respect to social and environmental safeguards; and
	  › Lack of analysis of actual physical progress against disbursements made under each contract and against plans.

Monitoring	Coordination meetings that were supposed to be held biannually and quarterly did not occur as scheduled.

Source: Office of Anticorruption and Integrity, Asian Development Bank.

Use of substandard materials and works that were substandard, defective, or off specifications. Executing and implementing agencies should ensure that contractors are adequately supervised and that any issues are addressed in a timely manner. The PIR asset inspection of ANR projects identified output defects, deviations from approved designs/specifications, and use of substandard materials, which could have been detected and rectified earlier had the project supervision been more robust. The inadequate supervision of contractors by supervision consultants and executing/implementing agencies resulted in delays, acceptance of works that were substandard, and cost overruns. Examples of related cases that the PIR team observed are in Table 9.

Table 9: Examples of the Use of Substandard Materials and Substandard, Defective, Off-Specification Works

Output Deficiency	Details
Substandard and off-specifications road works	**Onsite inspection revealed the following defects:** • Clear cover of culvert was inadequate; • Undulation was prevalent over the entire length of a road section, which may have been caused by improper base and sub-base course compaction; • Seal coat of asphalt concrete, supposedly 7 millimeters thick, was worn off exposing the asphalt concrete and, in some spots, even the asphalt concrete was worn off; • Poor quality of concrete, which may have been caused by inconsistent application of mix ratio; • Presence of moisture in wall and sunshade, which may have been caused by poor drainage system in the roof resulting in water clogging and subsequent seepage in the walls and other components of the building; • Cracks in walls due to inadequate brickwork or substandard materials used; • Poor gravel thickness, compaction, and/or material used, which would require premature maintenance; and • Missing turfing and/or trees, which were intended to prevent erosion.

Source: Office of Anticorruption and Integrity, Asian Development Bank.

CONTRACT AND ASSET MANAGEMENT

MITIGATING MEASURES
Output Monitoring Vulnerabilities

- Erring contractors, consultants, and suppliers should be held accountable to ensure that they fulfill their contractual obligations. This entails enforcing relevant penalty clauses and reporting poor performance to ADB without delay.

- For decentralized, complex, or high-risk projects, independent third-party monitoring firms should be engaged to augment the monitoring activities performed by executing

and/or implementing agencies, ADB regional departments, and supervision consultants.

- Executing/implementing agencies should closely monitor the supervision consultants. This entails rigorous review of the consultants' progress reports and, as necessary, verification of progress through field visits. A guide that provides a practical framework for field visits/ asset inspections can be accessed through this link: https://www.adb.org/sites/default/files/institutional-document/431571/asset-inspection-project-integrity.pdf.

FINANCIAL MANAGEMENT

ⓒ₁ Expenditure Management

Ineligible expenditures. Executing and implementing agencies should counter the risk of payments made for ineligible expenditures. Expenditures that are (i) not within the contract terms, (ii) inadequately or inappropriately supported, or (iii) unauthorized are considered ineligible. These indicate that claims were not thoroughly reviewed against contract provisions. They provide opportunities for fraud and expose the project to the risk of loss of funds. Examples of lapses in expenditure management are summarized in Table 10. Red flags indicative of integrity violations in expenditure management are summarized in Table 11.

Table 10: Examples of Ineligible Expenditures

Expenditure Category	Lapse/Gap in Expenditure
Contractors' progress billings	• A contractor received per diem reimbursements before a contract was awarded. • Contractors received payment for work that had not yet been conducted as recorded in the construction diaries or technical work acceptance minutes. • Some interim work certificates did not specify the quantity of works that had been completed or were not dated/signed by the supervision consultant, which signified that these were not reviewed and/or endorsed. • ADB proceeds were used or borrowed temporarily, in five project implementation units to pay ineligible expenses that should have been borne by the government.
Consultants' claims	**Inadequate verification of consultants' payment claims** The contract with a consulting firm specified that semiannual progress payments would be made following the submission of quarterly reports. However, although the firm submitted quarterly reports and statements of expenditures, its statement of expenditures lacked sufficient details, and expenses had no supporting documentation. There was no evidence that the project liaison office verified the firm's work or reviewed the financial schedules before endorsing the payments.
Project administration	**Inadequate verification of expense claims** Project liaison office made payments for non-project-related expenses and expenses with insufficient supporting documentation for vehicle maintenance, computer and photocopier expenses, per diem allowances, petrol, and mobile phone fees.

Source: Office of Anticorruption and Integrity, Asian Development Bank.

Table 11: Examples of Red Flags Indicative of Integrity Violations in Expenditure Management

FINANCIAL
MANAGEMENT

Type of Integrity Violation	Red Flags
Collusive practice	**Circumvention of contract variation approval thresholds** A contractor claimed expenses relating to a contract through an invoice for another contract. This was done by the contractor to avoid exceeding the 15% threshold for contract variations so as not to require higher approvals. The original contract amount would have increased by 21% if the required variation was considered. While both contracts had different contractors, they had the same authorized representative, who signed the bills for both contracts. The same authorized representative was also the representative of the contractors for two more related contracts (also indicative of fraudulent practice).
Fraudulent practice	**Undated, unnumbered, and reused cash memos** Numerous petty purchases were supported by undated cash memos at a project management office. The unnumbered and undated cash memos appeared to have been previously used as supporting documents and reused to support current purchases by the project management office. For example, there were 12 transactions from a store that were supported by the same cash memo, which were photocopied to support all 12 transactions.
Abuse	**Embezzlement: cash transfers to an entity with apparent connection with the project manager** On many occasions, a firm that was not a contractor or consultant for a project received funds from the project management unit. The firm's executive director, who was the accountant for other firms related to the project manager, withdrew the funds from the firm's bank account. These withdrawals were either by cash or checks payable to cash. Each of these withdrawals took place on the same day that the project management unit sent funds to the firm.

Notes: 1. Collusive practice is an arrangement between two or more parties designed to achieve an improper purpose, including influencing improperly the actions of another party.
2. Fraudulent practice is any act or omission, including a misrepresentation, that knowingly or recklessly misleads, or attempts to mislead, a party to obtain a financial or other benefit or to avoid an obligation.
3. Abuse is theft, waste, or improper use of assets related to ADB-related activity, either committed intentionally or through reckless disregard.

Source: Office of Anticorruption and Integrity, Asian Development Bank.

MITIGATING MEASURES
Ineligible Expenditures

- Before endorsing claims for payment, executing and implementing agencies should ensure that (i) payment approval procedures are followed, (ii) supporting documents are checked for accuracy and completeness, and (iii) details in the claims are validated against the contracts and supporting documents. Payments should be refused or reduced in line with relevant contractual provisions for works or services that were not performed or goods that were not delivered (a checklist on how to avoid common errors/lapses in expenditure payment processing is on Checklist 2).

- ADB regional departments and resident missions should ensure that executing and implementing agencies, including project implementing units/offices, understand their obligations under ADB's Anticorruption Policy, especially the obligation to report any integrity violations to OAI without delay when they are initially identified or suspected.

PROCUREMENT

CONTRACT
AND ASSET
MANAGEMENT

**FINANCIAL
MANAGEMENT**

OTHER
VULNERABILITIES

Checklist 2: How to Avoid Common Errors and Lapses in Expenditure Payment Processing

All Types

☐ Verify the claim against the milestone payment terms stipulated in the contract (including contract variations).

☐ Check whether the payment information indicated in the claim matches with the payment information in the contract.

☐ Identify any red flags on the supporting documents submitted, e.g., erasures, alterations, or other errors and ask for clarifications.

Works (Contractors)

☐ Verify the claim against interim payment certificates/certificates of completion. Check if there are claims on non-workdays (work on a weekend or holiday with no preapproval).

Services (Consultants)

☐ Verify the remuneration claim (for input-based contracts) against detailed timesheets submitted.

☐ Verify claims for reimbursable expenses against supporting documents as required in the contract (not applicable for full lump-sum contracts), including:
  ○ Travel costs—proof of travel (tickets, receipts, boarding passes);
  ○ Accommodation—proof of stay (hotel bills, invoices, receipts); and
  ○ Seminars and workshops—attendance sheets, invoices or receipts for workshop costs like venue and equipment rental and refreshments.

Goods (Suppliers)

☐ Verify the claim against sales invoice and delivery receipt/proof that goods have been delivered, inspected, accepted, and, as necessary, properly installed.

Note: Where a red flag is identified, refer it to OAI for further verification.
Source: Office of Anticorruption and Integrity, Asian Development Bank.

◇C2 Financial Reporting

Inadequate and unreliable accounting systems. To ensure that financial information is provided in a timely and accurate manner for project implementation and progress monitoring purposes, executing/implementing agencies should maintain adequate and reliable project accounting systems and apply accounting standards acceptable to ADB. Inadequate and unreliable systems increase (i) the risk of undetected integrity violations, noncompliance, and other irregularities; and (ii) the risk of making unsound project management decisions based on faulty financial information. Examples of accounting systems and procedures deficiencies are summarized in Table 12.

Table 12: Examples of Accounting System Deficiencies

Accounting System Aspect	Deficiency
Financial records	• The project management units (PMUs) failed to maintain essential books of accounts such as (i) receipts and disbursement ledger, (ii) bank control, (iii) value-added tax (VAT) control, (iv) advance control, and (v) petty cash ledger, as required under the project accounting manual. Instead, only a check issue register was maintained. • The PMUs did not maintain records (i) to monitor VAT input that had been paid and (ii) to keep track of VAT refunds on the ADB and the cofinancier's portion of funding.
Account reconciliations	• PMUs did not perform regular bank reconciliations. • Material discrepancies between the project financial statement and annual statement of sources and uses of funds had not been reconciled for at least 3 years, undermining the accuracy and reliability of the project financial reports.
Segregation of duties	• The functions of accountant and cashier were performed by the same individual. ⚠ • The accountant who assisted in project-related financial activities also prepared accounting books and checks, performed bank reconciliations, and signed checks. ⚠
Transaction accounting	• Expenditures that were capital in nature were recorded as expenses. • Utilization of goods purchased was not recorded, i.e., transfer from the inventory asset account to the related expense account.

Legend: ⚠ = indicative of potential conflict of interest. Conflict of interest is any situation in which a party has interests that could improperly influence a party's performance of official duties or responsibilities, contractual obligations, or compliance with applicable laws and regulations.

Source: Office of Anticorruption and Integrity, Asian Development Bank.

MITIGATING MEASURES
Inadequate and Unreliable Accounting Systems

The executing agency should (i) develop appropriate policies and procedures on maintaining adequate and reliable accounting systems, (ii) train all the project management agencies/units/offices on implementing the policies and procedures, and (iii) monitor their compliance with the policies and procedures.

The policies and procedures should include guidelines on maintaining financial records, performing account reconciliations, establishing segregation of duties, and accounting for project transactions. For this purpose, the executing agency is encouraged to implement a computerized accounting system, which would facilitate semi-automation of data entry and transactions reviews, and real-time data generation.

PROCUREMENT

CONTRACT
AND ASSET
MANAGEMENT

FINANCIAL
MANAGEMENT

**OTHER
VULNERABILITES**

OTHER INTEGRITY-RELATED VULNERABILITIES THAT CUT ACROSS PROJECT IMPLEMENTATION PROCESSES

Integrity risks in project implementation principally result from the executing/implementing agency's capacity gaps—particularly in procurement, contract and asset management, financial management processes, and project record maintenance.

D1 Executing and Implementing Agencies' Capacity

Inadequate technical capacity on ADB operational guidelines and procedures. Project staff of executing and implementing agencies should be knowledgeable on ADB procurement, financial management, and disbursement guidelines and procedures. Given the observed frequent staff turnover and high dependence on consultants, executing and implementing agencies should ensure that this institutional knowledge is retained, transferred, and refreshed.

MITIGATING MEASURES
Staff Capacity Issues

To ensure that institutional knowledge and practices over ADB operational guidelines and procedures are retained, transferred, and refreshed, executing and implementing agencies with assistance from ADB as necessary, should develop an onboarding kit for new staff that includes primers and manuals. Regular relevant trainings should be undertaken for all staff and a quality assurance or monitoring process should be implemented under the guidance of or with assistance from ADB as required.

D2 Records Management

Inadequate records management system. Inaccurate or incomplete audit trail of project activities complicates the timely prevention and detection of integrity violations, noncompliance, and errors. Executing and implementing agencies should maintain an effective records management system that evidences their compliance with anticorruption, procurement, financial management, and other relevant guidelines.

MITIGATING MEASURES
Records Management Issues

Executing and implementing agencies should establish and maintain an effective system of records management to (i) facilitate records identification, validation, storage, and retrieval; (ii) improve accountability; (iii) drive timely detection of errors and irregularities; and (iv) prevent misplacement.

CONCLUSION

Through its proactive integrity reviews of 14 agriculture, natural resources, and rural development projects, ADB's Office of Anticorruption and Integrity identified vulnerabilities and red flags in (i) procurement, (ii) contract and asset management, and (iii) financial management processes. Key vulnerabilities are summarized in Table 13.

To manage related risks, ADB encourages project staff to apply the mitigating measures recommended in this publication and use the due diligence checklists for bid evaluation (Checklist 1) and expenditure payment processing (Checklist 2). Project staff must remain alert to red flags of integrity violations and report suspected violations to the Office of Anticorruption and Integrity.

Integrity risks are generally elevated in complex, decentralized projects (i.e., large-scale projects involving numerous project components, geographical locations, and implementing entities). These projects benefit from strong accountability and control mechanisms that clarify responsibilities at each implementation level (from the executing agency down to the last implementing unit), and from closer supervision by the executing agency and ADB. Integrity-related controls should be embedded in contracts, manuals, and other authoritative documents.

Under Operational Priority 7 of Strategy 2030, ADB has committed to support governments in their efforts to eradicate corruption and to implement anticorruption measures in all its projects and programs. We trust that the insights compiled in this publication will contribute to these endeavors.

Table 13: High- and Medium-Risk Vulnerabilities and their Implications

Process	Subprocess	Vulnerability	Risk Implication
Procurement	**A1 Bidding**	Collusion among bidders, fraudulent practice, and unmanaged conflicts of interest	Conflicts of interest, fraud, and corruption jeopardizing the project and alienating prospective bidders
		Deficiencies in sales of bidding documents and bid submission registers	Diminished transparency and fairness as a potential qualified bidder may not submit a responsive bid due to nonreceipt of important bidding information
		Deficient and inconsistent information in bidding documents	Subjective or incorrect evaluations resulting in contract awards to unqualified bidders
	A2 Bid evaluation	Inadequate due diligence by bid evaluation committees	Diminished transparency and fairness of the bid evaluation process resulting in contract awards to unqualified bidders
	A3 Contract award	Deficient performance securities	Uncompensated delays and losses caused by erring contractors or suppliers
Contract and asset management	**B1 Contract administration**	Deficient securities and insurance	Uncompensated losses caused by erring contractors or suppliers and damages or losses on project assets
	B2 Output monitoring	Deficiencies in the reporting of a project's implementation progress	Implementation delays and cost overruns resulting from implementation problems that were left undisclosed or unaddressed
		Use of substandard materials and acceptance of works that were substandard, defective, or off specifications resulting from the inadequate monitoring of contractors by executing/ implementing agencies and supervision consultants	Implementation delays, inferior quality of outputs, and cost overruns
Financial management	**C1 Expenditure management**	Ineligible, unsupported, or inaccurate expenditures being paid resulting from weaknesses in the review and analysis of claims	Heightened opportunities for fraud resulting in potential loss of project funds; potential threat to subsequent maintenance or warranty claims
	C2 Financial reporting	Inadequate and unreliable accounting systems	Greater risk of not detecting integrity violations, noncompliance, or other irregularities
			Flawed project management decisions based on inaccurate financial information

Source: Office of Anticorruption and Integrity, Asian Development Bank.

APPENDIX List of Proactive Integrity Reviews of Agriculture, Natural Resources, and Rural Development Projects

Country	Project	PIR Report Issuance Date
Afghanistan	Water Resources Development Investment Program—Project 1	May 2020
Bangladesh	Forestry Sector Project	Sep 2005
	Second Rural Infrastructure Improvement Project	Aug 2011
Cambodia	Northwest Rural Development Project	Aug 2006
People's Republic of China	Ningxia Integrated Ecosystem and Agricultural Development Project	Jun 2014
Indonesia	Poor Farmers' Income Improvement through Innovation Project	Dec 2007
Kyrgyz Republic	Agriculture Area Development Project	Dec 2008
Lao People's Democratic Republic	Sustainable Natural Resource Management and Productivity Enhancement Project	Apr 2014
Mongolia	Cadastral Survey and Land Registration	Jan 2006 Jan 2010
Nepal	Decentralized Rural Infrastructure and Livelihood Project	Apr 2012
Pakistan	Malakand Rural Development Project	Jun 2007
Philippines	Infrastructure for Rural Productivity Enhancement Sector Project	Apr 2010
Philippines	Integrated Coastal Resources Management Project	Mar 2013 Dec 2015 (follow-up)
Viet Nam	Rural Infrastructure Project	Jan 2005

Note: Publication of full proactive integrity review reports started in 2008. Proactive integrity review reports prior to 2008 published on the Asian Development Bank website only contain report abstracts/summaries.

ADB placed on hold its assistance in Afghanistan effective 15 August 2021. ADB Statement on Afghanistan | Asian Development Bank (published on 10 November 2021). Manila.

Source: Office of Anticorruption and Integrity, Asian Development Bank.